About BLAST OFF!

This handbook is Unit VI in a uniquely developed multidisciplinary series created with the elementary student, the teacher, the librarian, and the curriculum in mind. Called "Guided Research Discovery Units," the series includes six self-contained handbooks, each presenting a number of reproducible activity units related to a particular curriculum area:

Unit I   ANIMALS! ANIMALS! ANIMALS! *(Natural Science)*
Unit II   IT'S A SMALL WORLD! *(Geography)*
Unit III   FASCINATING PEOPLE! *(History)*
Unit IV   FUN PAC! *(Language Arts)*
Unit V   BOOKSHELF ADVENTURES *(Children's Literature)*
Unit VI   BLAST OFF! *(Space Science)*

Through the completely organized, directed research projects in each handbook, students and teachers are introduced to universally appealing topics that can be explored by each individual at his or her own level of competency and speed. Each project focuses on finding certain facts, recording the facts, and rewriting the facts in sentence form. Every page of each project is designed differently to entice, captivate, or stimulate the students involved in research/reference work.

BLAST OFF! includes four projects suggested for students ages 10-14. Each of them can be used effectively to:

- develop a unit of study
- supplement a unit of study
- develop language, research, and reading skills through an interesting topic that may be, but is not necessarily, curriculum-related
- assist the teacher or librarian in organizing his or her presentation to the class or individual students before actual use of the projects
- promote creativity instead of copying in reference/research work
- provide meaningful and challenging activities for the gifted or enthusiastic individual working beyond the classroom environment
- extend or culminate research skills already taught in the classroom or resource center
- motivate students who are "turned off" to working on research/reference projects

The all-inclusive "Teacher's Guide" enables you as a teacher or librarian to use these projects in a variety of ways so that they will prove to be a most valuable asset to your school program.

Nancy M. Hall
Ruth V. Snoddon

About the Authors

Ruth V. Snoddon, M.A., Northern Michigan University (Marquette), B.A., Laurentian University (Sudbury, Ontario), has been involved in elementary education for the past 24 years as a classroom teacher and as a librarian. She has worked with curriculum committees, presented workshops on professional development, and compiled a policy manual for school library resource centers.

Nancy M. Hall, B.A., Laurentian University, has taught for 14 years and has experience in the library and in the classroom. Recently, she developed a language arts course of study for her school. Mrs. Hall is presently working on her M.A. in elementary education at Northern Michigan University.

Table of Contents

Teacher's Guide: *Pages*
    Suggestions for Use 5
    Research and Language Skills 5
    Bibliography 6
    Displaying Students' Work 7
    How to Make a Simple Mobile 8
    Above and Beyond 10

Research Projects:

Title	*Key*	
ONE GIANT STEP	VI — G1-10	11
OUR SOLAR SYSTEM	VI — S1-13	22
STAR TRACK	VI — T1-9	36
WEATHER	VI — W1-11	46

Teacher's Guide

The student projects in this Guided Research Unit can be used in a variety of ways. They require little or no preparation time other than that needed to duplicate the project outline pages for students. The contents are all inclusive and self-explanatory.

In the following, you will find specific suggestions for using the projects with your students, a listing of some of the reference/research and language skills developed by these activities, and guidelines for teaching students correct bibliographic form. Also included are directions for displaying students' finished work and ideas for additional project-related activities.

Suggestions for Use

The projects in each Discovery Unit can be used by individual students, small groups, or an entire class. They can also be used by an entire class divided into three or four groups (one group doing Star Track, another Weather, etc.) or by several pupils working on one project, with each assigned to do part and the completed work displayed as a cooperative effort.

Teachers and librarians can use the projects in many different ways, for example, as:

- a method for covering a particular subject area using the project as a guide for organizing a specific topic
- a group project for some, while other students work on the same topic using other ideas
- an extension or culmination of reference skills being taught within the classroom or resource center
- an enrichment program for individual students or groups of students working beyond the classroom environment
- a guide to note-taking

For instance, younger students in grades 2 or 3 might take notes cooperatively with teacher assistance and then use the project pages to write their notes on. Their completed project can be mounted on backing, made into a mobile or booklet, or displayed as the teacher desires.

Research and Language Skills

The following is just a partial listing of the research and language skills that are developed in these projects:

1. Following of printed directions
2. Focusing on a narrow topic that can be covered, e.g., *WEATHER—CLOUDS—NIMBUS*

3. Knowledge of some parts of books, e.g., title page and table of contents, and use of the index
4. Use of the card catalog (Author, Title, and Subject cards) and library organization (Dewey Decimal System and physical arrangement)
5. Searching out and locating relevant data from a wide variety of sources, i.e., encyclopedias, books, pictures, filmstrips, pamphlets, tapes, etc.
6. Selecting the most appropriate sources from materials gathered
7. Noting sources of information (Bibliography), i.e., Encyclopedia, Title(s), Volume No., Page No., Call No., and Other Sources. (*Note:* See the following section for a more extensive bibliographic form to use with the projects.)
8. Skimming for specific information from all sources used, with the focus on main ideas and key words
9. Writing the specific information collected in *note form* under appropriate headings on the outline provided (categorizing and summarizing)
10. Using gathered information from the outline and rewriting it in proper *sentence* and *paragraph* structure with emphasis on correct grammar and spelling

Bibliography

Beginning in the third or fourth grade, the young researcher should be taught and encouraged to use correct bibliographic form. There are three main pieces of information in a bibliography: the person (author, editor, performer), the title, and information regarding publication (city, publisher, and the copyright or publication date). The three sections are separated by periods. Titles of selections from an encyclopedia or a magazine appear within quotation marks. The second line of an entry is always indented. The items are arranged in alphabetical order and are numbered.

The teacher may use some discretion in abbreviating or adapting the format to local style. Bibliographic forms and examples follow.

Books

Author. *Title*. City of publication: Publisher, Copyright.

Examples:

1. Knight, Clayton. *Big Book of Helicopters*. New York: Grosset & Dunlap, Inc., 1971.
2. Sikorsky, Igor. *Story of the Winged-S*. New York: Dodd, Mead & Co., 1967.
3. Taylor, Michael J., & Taylor, John W. *Helicopters of the World*. New York: Charles Scribner's Sons, 1979.

Encyclopedia Articles

"Article." *Encyclopedia name*, Last copyright, Volume number, Page(s).

Example:

1. "Helicopter." *Encyclopedia Britannica*, 1972, 11, 314-316.

Teacher's Guide 7

Magazine and Newspaper Articles

Author (if known). "Article." *Magazine*, Volume number (Date), Page(s).

Example:

1. Weaver, Kenneth F. "The Incredible Universe." *National Geographic,* 145 (May 1974), 589.

Records, Tapes, Filmstrips

Title of Strip. (Filmstrip). Producer, Copyright (if available).

Example:

1. *War for Independence Bunker Hill* (Filmstrip). Encyclopedia Britannica Films, Inc., 1962.

Displaying Students' Work

Each guided research project in this unit has been developed so that students' work can be displayed in several forms. Suggestions for the most appropriate form of display are included with the particular project. Teachers, librarians, and students can also adopt other forms if they so desire.

The completed project can be:

- Mounted on a 24″ × 18″ piece of backing and displayed on a classroom bulletin board or elsewhere

- Made into a booklet

- Displayed as a mobile, as described in the next section

How to Make a Simple Mobile

Here are the materials and step-by-step directions for constructing a simple mobile with the project outlines.

You will need:

    2 sturdy plastic drinking straws
    lightweight yarn or string
    backing (construction paper or light bristol board)
    scissors
    glue
    paper puncher

Follow these steps to construct the mobile:

1. Glue the project shapes to the backing.

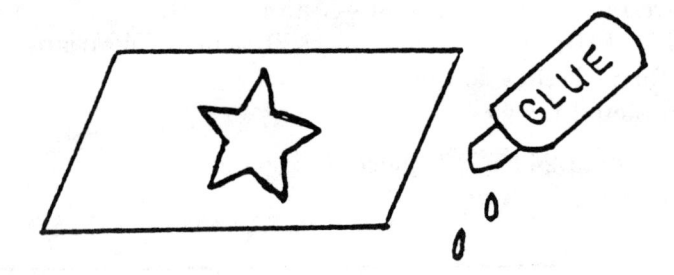

2. When the glue dries, cut out the shapes.

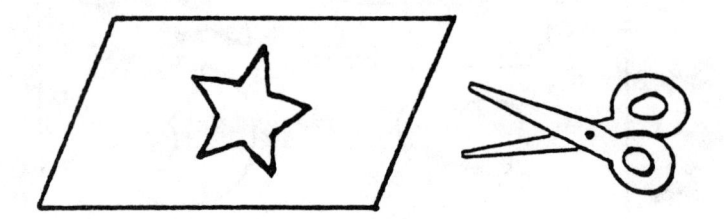

3. Punch a hole at the suitable location on each outline.

Teacher's Guide

4. Attach a string of varied length (from 24" to 30") to each shape and make a large knot at the end of each piece of string.

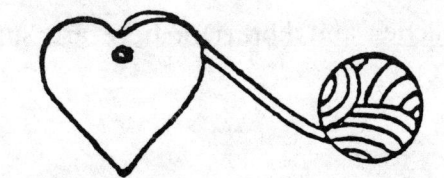

5. *Firmly* bind the straws together with yarn or string in the form of a cross.

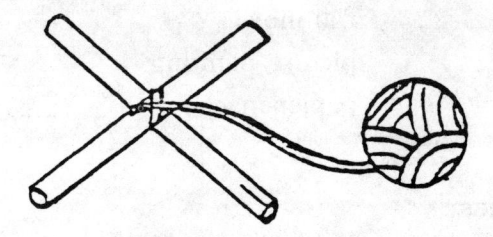

6. Cut a 1" slit in the end of each straw and fasten each string by sliding the yarn through the slit below the knot (or just tie the string on firmly).
7. Tie string at the center of the crosspieces to suspend the mobile from the ceiling. Adjust the straws to balance the mobile evenly.
8. If desired, add the project title in whatever way desired.

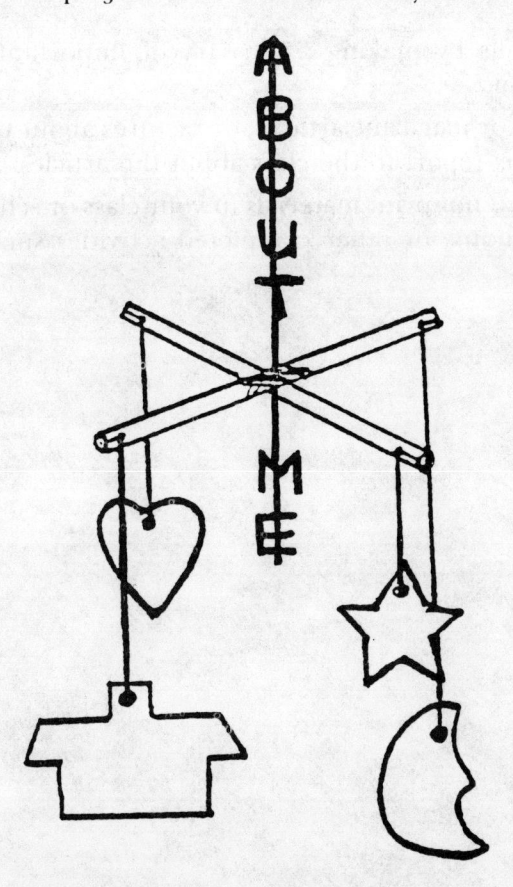

Above and Beyond

For the creative teacher and librarian, here are suggestions for other project-related activities.

Art Activities

pipe cleaner figures	sculptures
murals	TV programs
dioramas	collages
modeling	roll movies
puppets	picture painting
filmstrips	papier-mâché
soap carvings	

Language Arts Activities

1. Write a newscast or become a reporter or interviewer for your class.
2. Write a story or a poem to go with your topic.
3. Read a fiction story related to your topic and write a book report, diary or journal entry about it.
4. Learn how to spell and pronounce new words found in research materials you are using.
5. Use dictionary skills by making a glossary of important and unusual words related to your topic.
6. Collect newspaper or magazine articles, or pictures about your topic. Make these into a scrapbook or report to the class about the articles or pictures.
7. Display all print and nonprint materials in your class or school for others to view, i.e., articles from home or other completed activities such as those previously listed.

VI — G

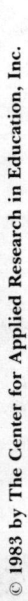

ONE GIANT STEP

1. Check the sources you could use for this topic; for example, books, encyclopedias, filmstrips, pictures, and so on. Magazines and newspapers could be useful. Choose at least four sources and list them on Bibliography page VI — G2.

2. Study your project pages. Read and collect the information you need. Write the information in NOTE FORM on outline chart VI — G3.

3. When you have gathered all your facts, rewrite your information on the outline pages. Use proper SENTENCES. Check for spelling or grammar errors. Use markers, crayons, or colored pencils in suitable colors to outline your pictures.

4. Cut out the outlines and glue them on construction paper. Make your space travel unit into a booklet, a mobile, or a chart.

5. See your teacher about making a SUPER EFFORT.

6. Present your work to the class as your teacher suggests.

7. APPROXIMATE TIME TO COMPLETE PROJECT: 6 — 10 hours.

BIBLIOGRAPHY　　　　　　　　　　　　　　　　　　　　　　　　　　　　　　VI — G2

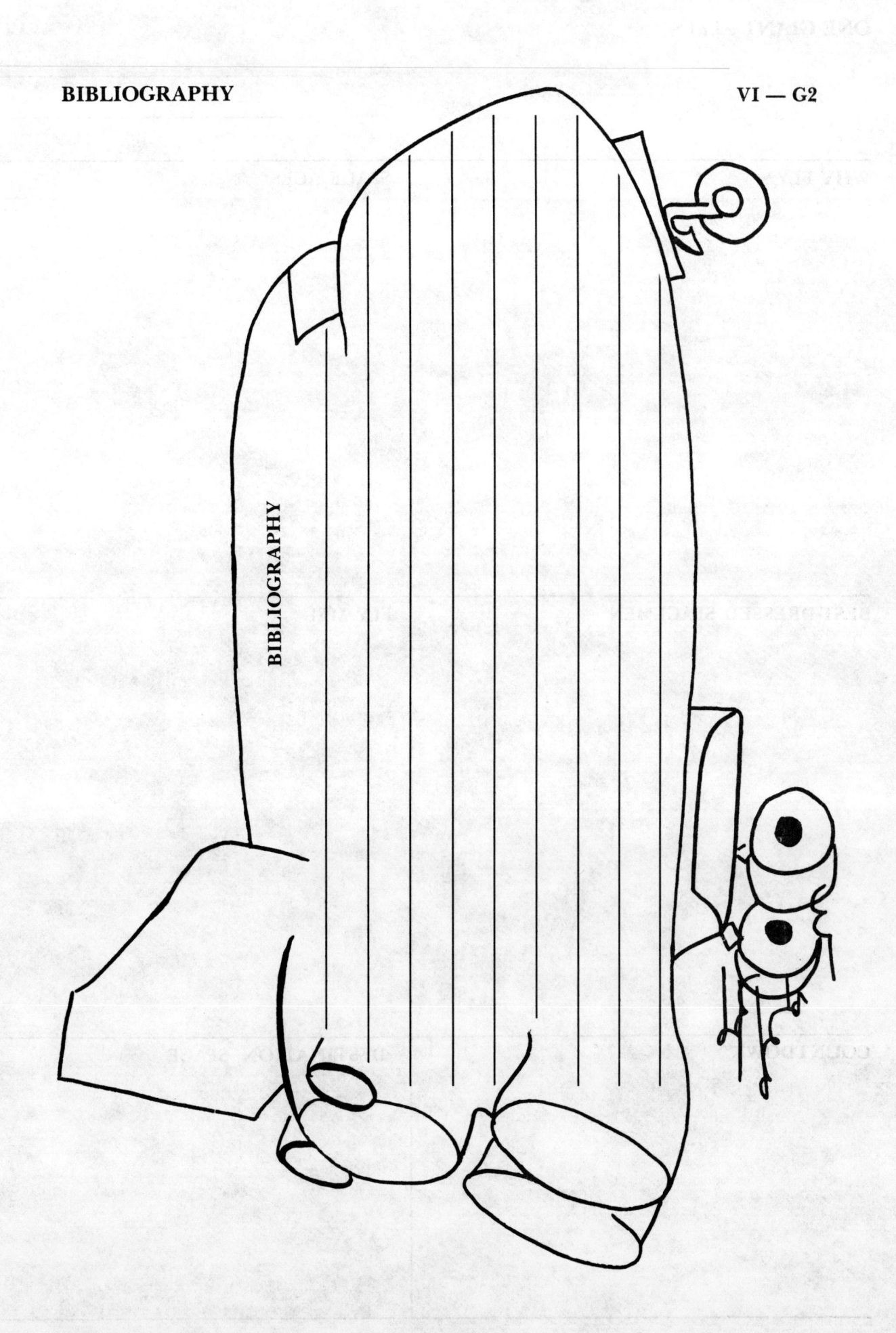

ONE GIANT STEP

VI — G3

Name _____

Date _____

WHY FLY?	SPACE ACES
BEST-DRESSED SPACEMEN	FLY ME!
COUNTDOWN	DESTINATION: SPACE

WHY FLY? VI — G4

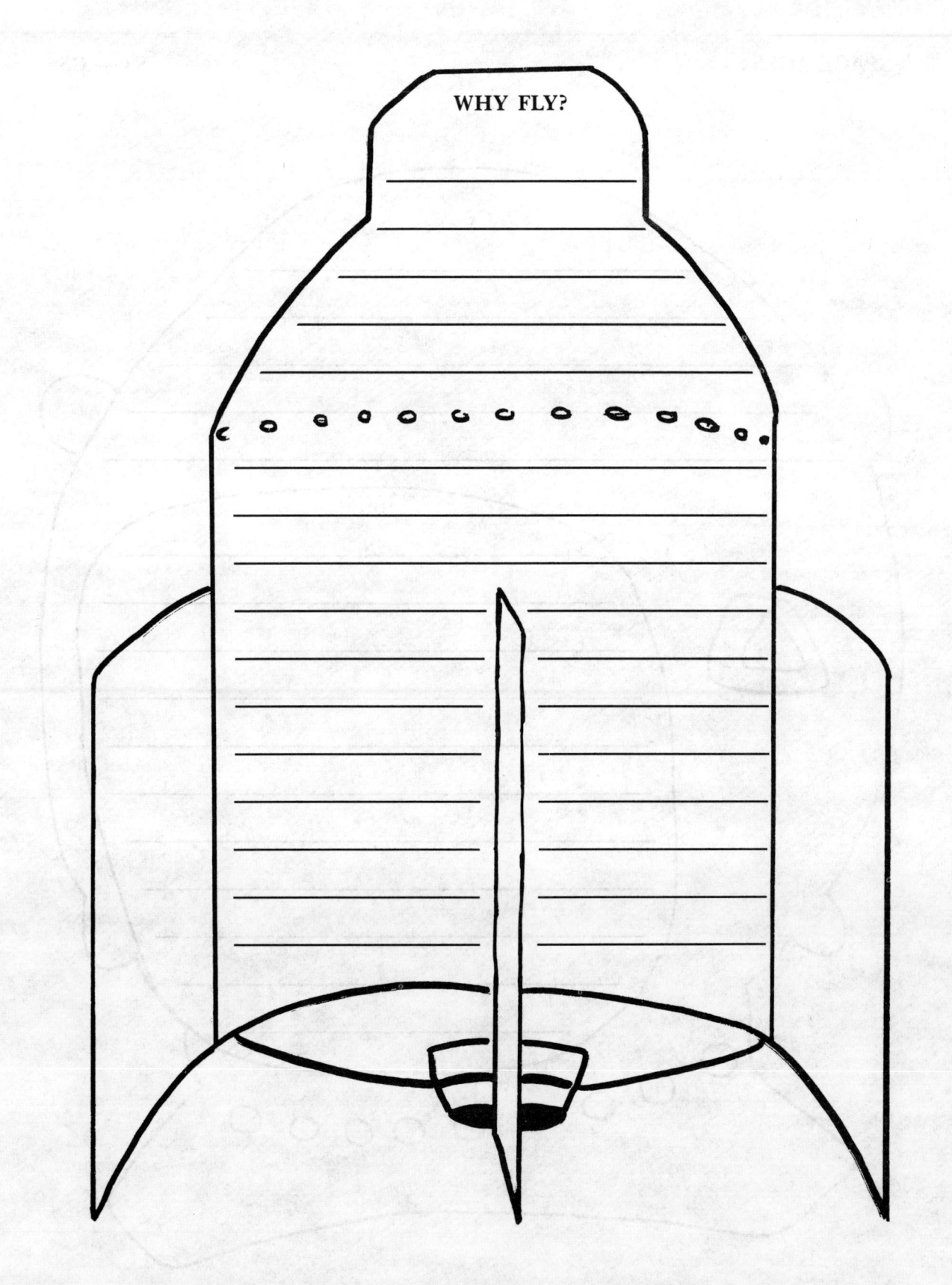

WHY FLY?

What reasons does mankind have for exploring space?

SPACE ACES

SPACE ACES

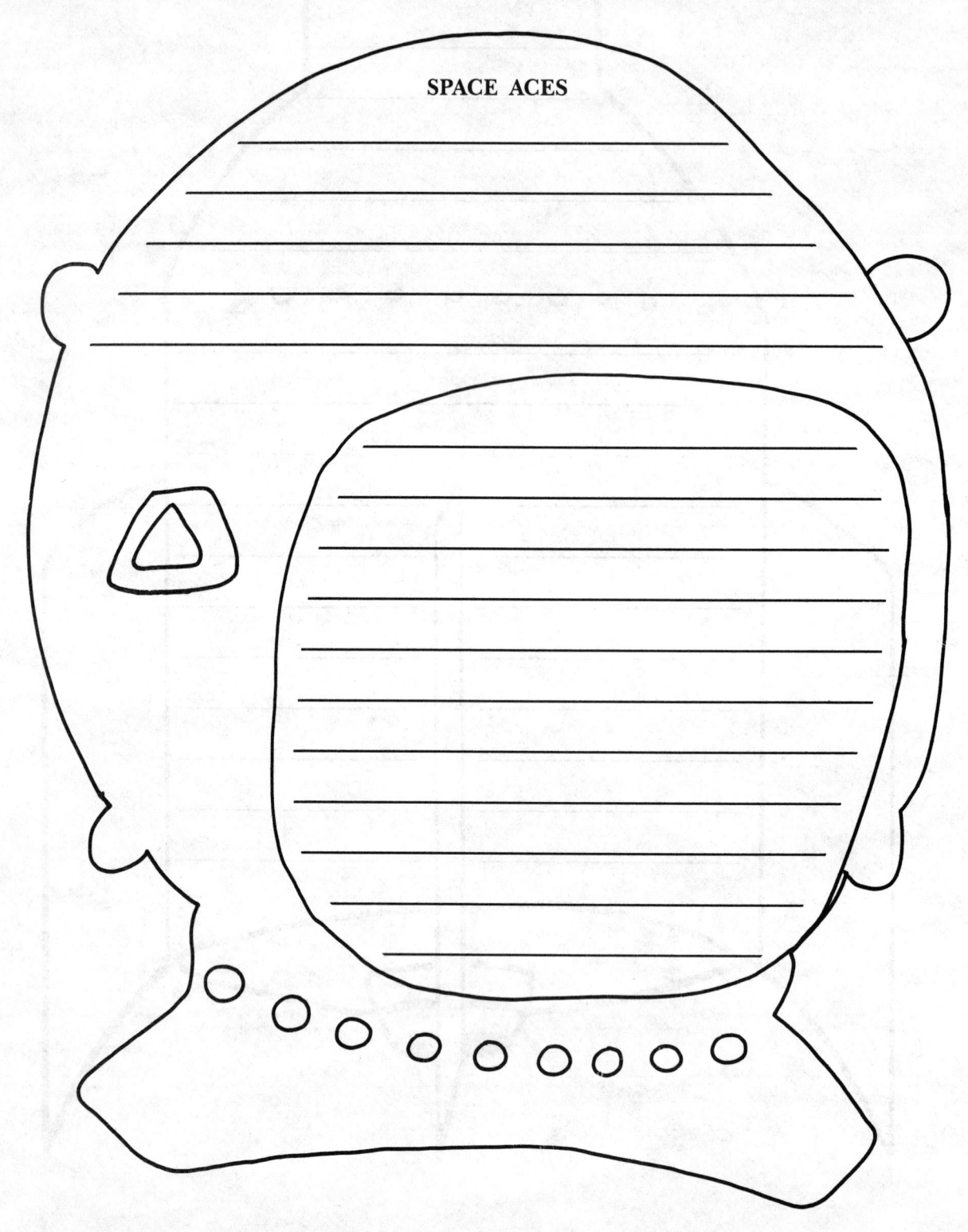

Who were the first man and the first woman in space? What countries were first to explore space flight?

BEST-DRESSED SPACEMEN VI — G6

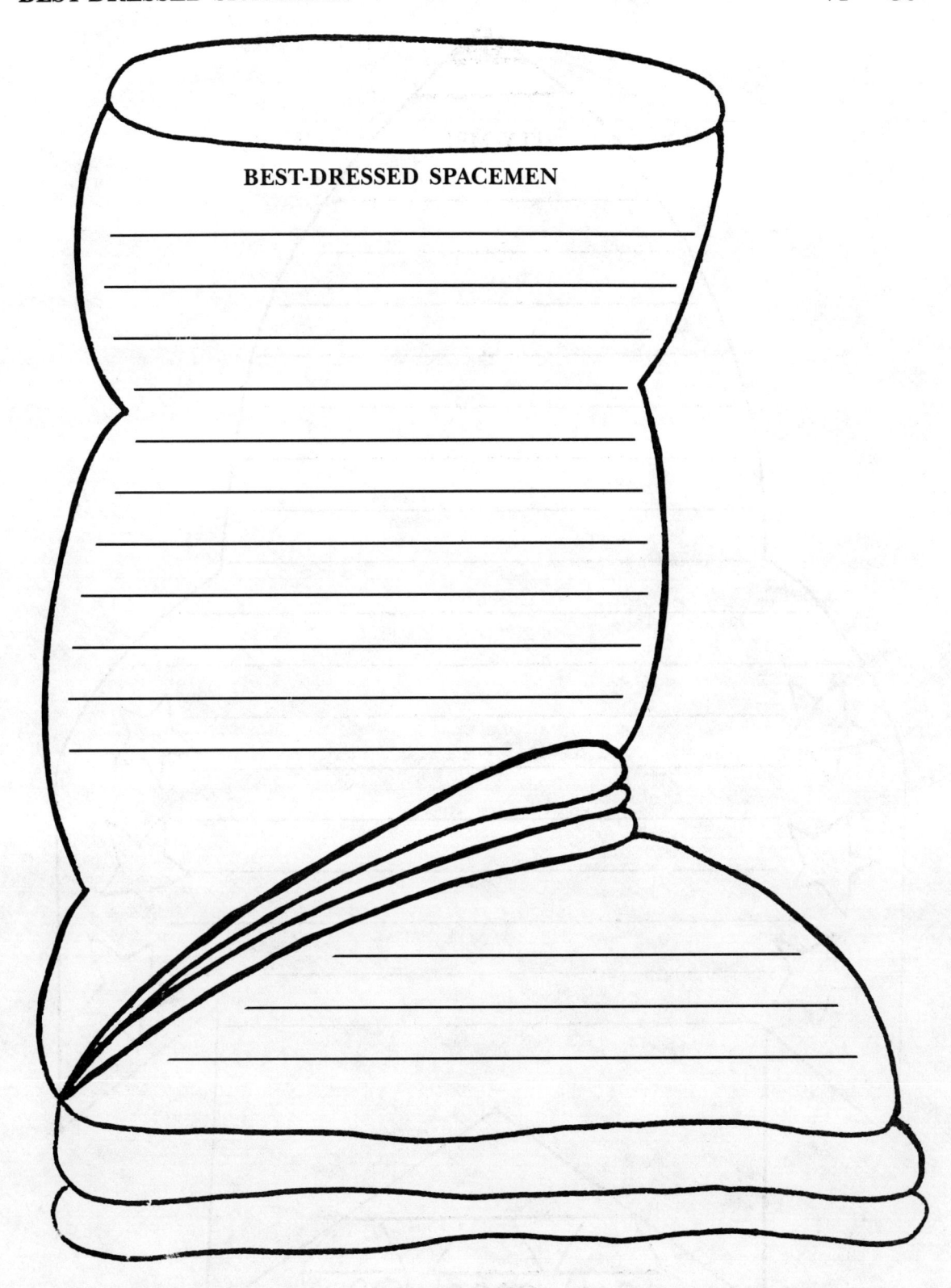

BEST-DRESSED SPACEMEN

What special clothing and/or equipment do people need for space travel?

FLY ME!

FLY ME!

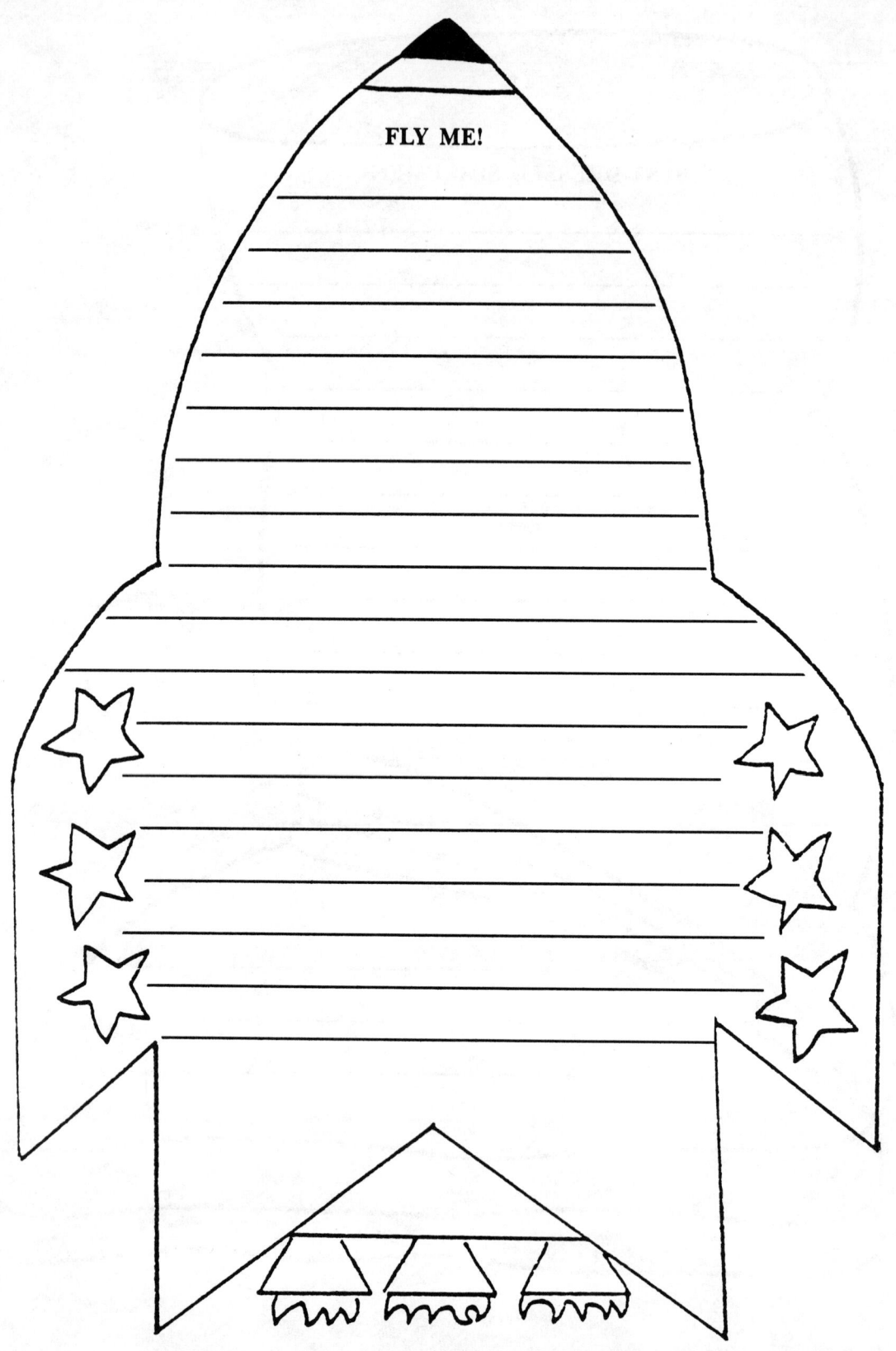

Tell about the different types of space vehicles.

COUNTDOWN

VI — G8

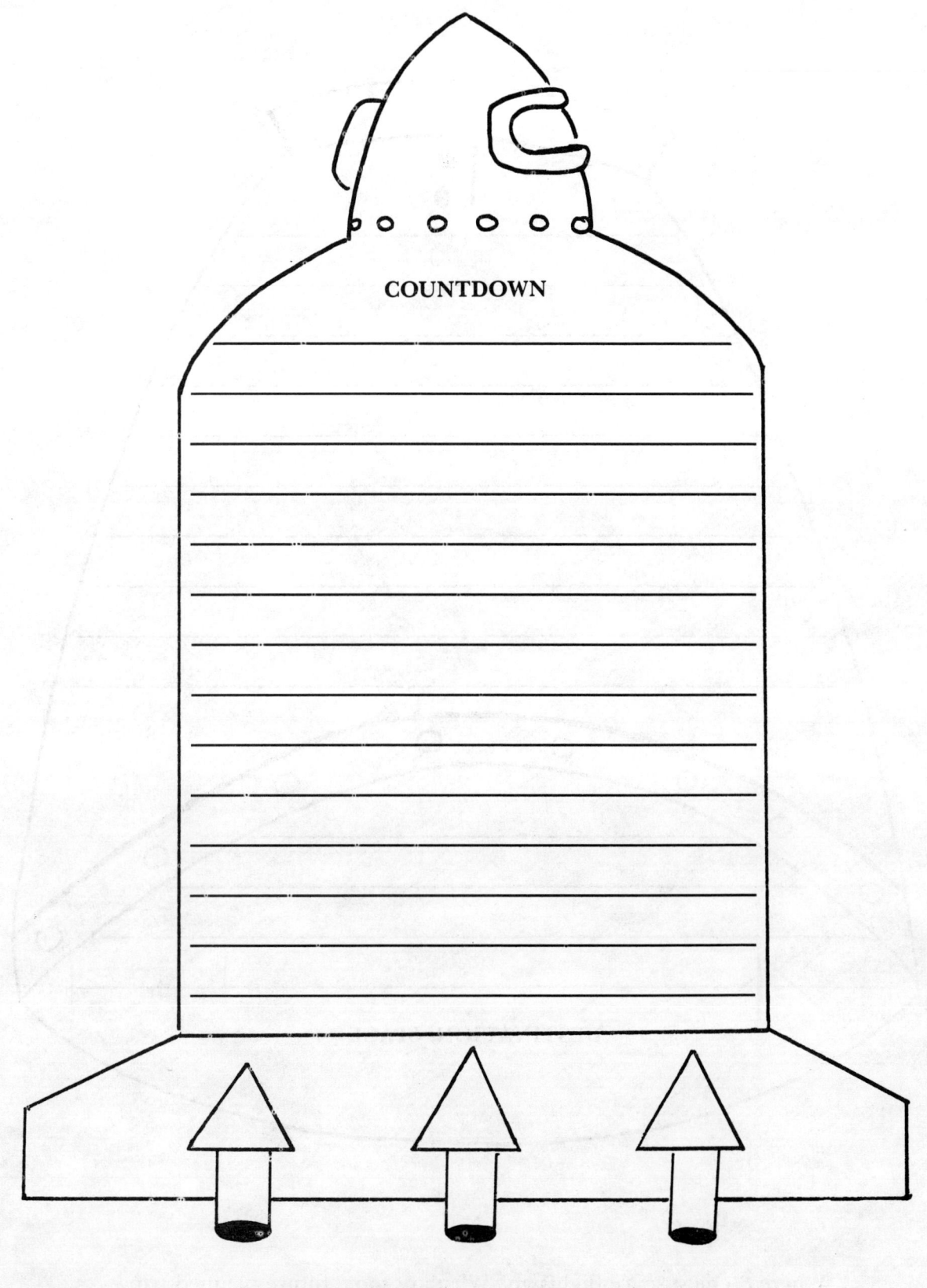

COUNTDOWN

When did mankind first enter space?

DESTINATION: SPACE　　　　　　　　　　　　　　　　　　　　　VI — G9

DESTINATION: SPACE

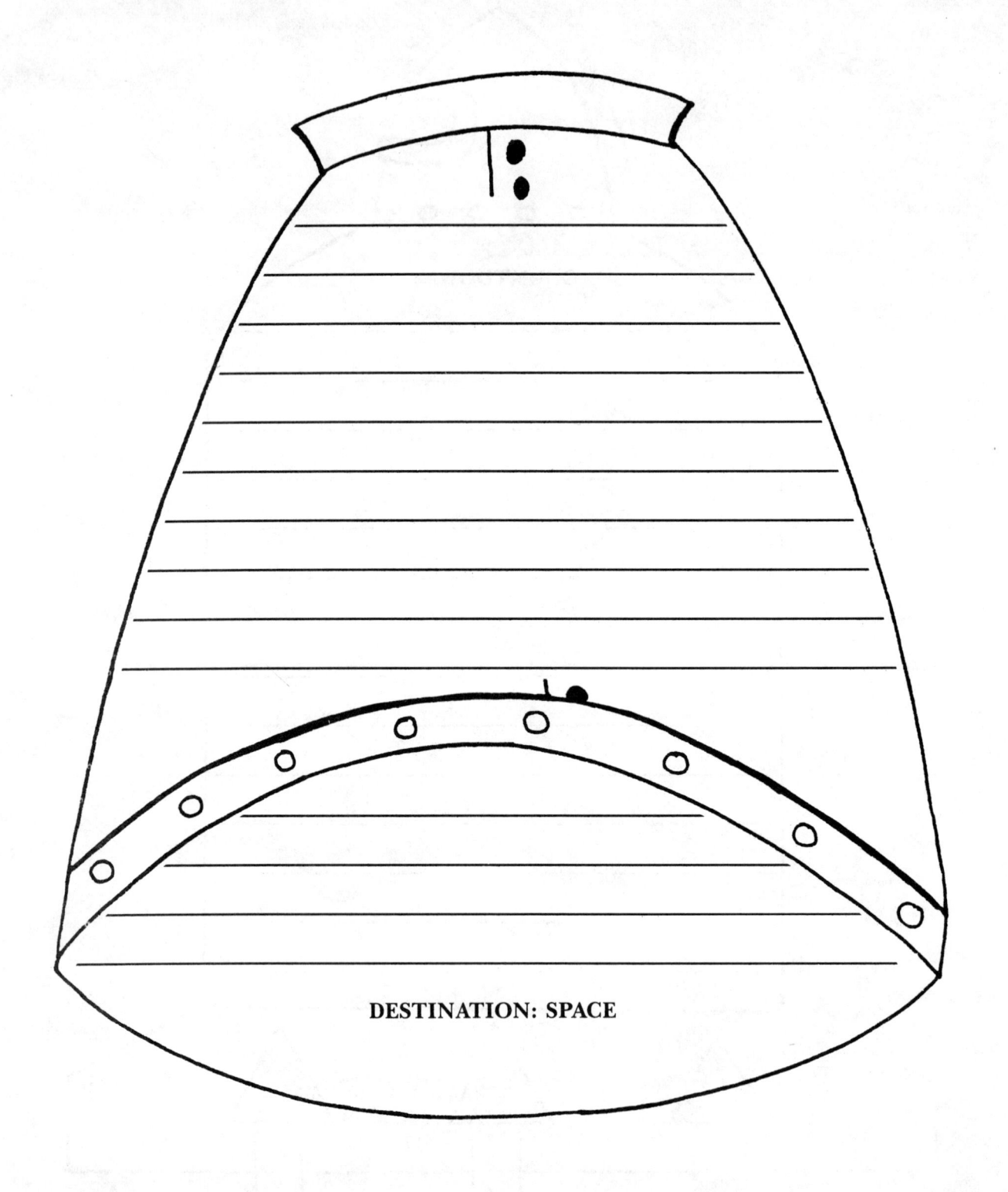

Where do most space flights go? What are some future planned trips?

SUPER EFFORT   VI — G10

1. Choose a famous person involved with space flight. Find out about this person. Pretend *you* are this person and let your classmates interview you.

2. Make a model of a rocket, a satellite, or a space station. Explain it to your classmates.

3. Use a small action figure or model and make a spacesuit for it. Use cloth, foil, plastics, and other materials.

4. Make large labeled wall charts to illustrate a rocket, a spacesuit, and other space topics.

5. What are some of the problems and/or dangers of space travel? Report on them.

6. Make and narrate a roll movie of a rocket launching.

7. Hundreds of years ago people were thinking and dreaming of flying. Who were some of these early "spacemen" and how did they plan on "blasting off"?

OUR SOLAR SYSTEM

VI—S

© 1983 by The Center for Applied Research in Education, Inc.

OUR SOLAR SYSTEM   VI — S1

1. Check the sources you could use for this topic, for example: books, encyclopedias, filmstrips, and pictures. Choose at least *four* sources and list them on Bibliography page VI — S2.

2. Read and collect information about the planets. Look for information on the size, distance from the sun, appearance, surface conditions, atmosphere, moons, etc. Write the information in NOTE FORM on outline chart VI — S3.

3. When you have gathered all your facts, rewrite your information on the planet outlines. Use proper SENTENCES. Check for spelling or grammar errors. Use markers, crayons, or colored pencils in suitable colors to outline and color your pictures.

4. Cut out the outlines and glue them on construction paper. Make your planet study unit into a booklet, a mobile, or a chart. At this time you could also cut out the correct number of moons for each planet.

5. See your teacher about making a SUPER EFFORT.

6. Present your work to the class as your teacher suggests.

7. APPROXIMATE TIME TO COMPLETE PROJECT: 6 — 10 hours.

BIBLIOGRAPHY

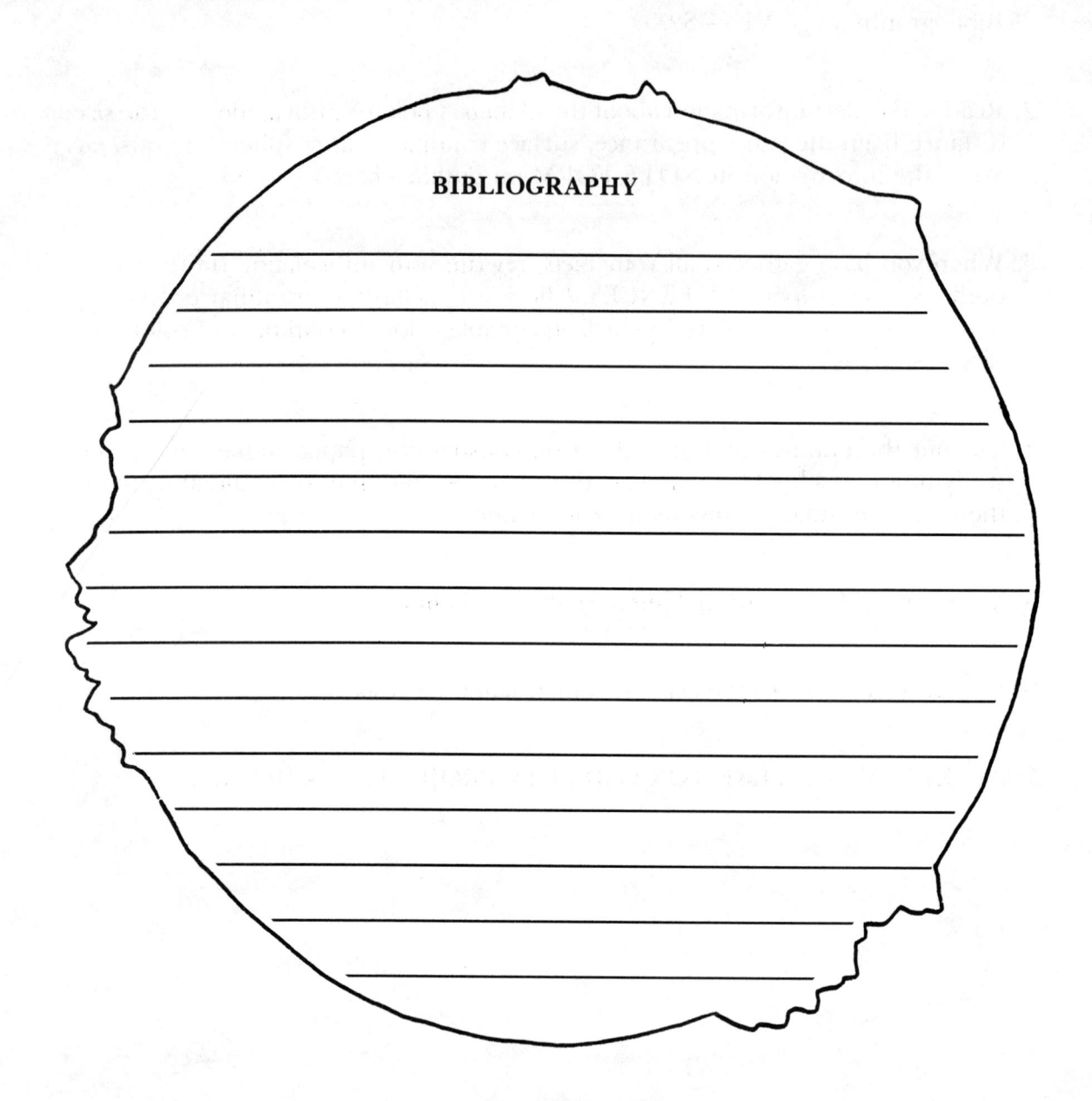

OUR SOLAR SYSTEM

VI — S3

Name _____

Date _____

THE PLANETS

EARTH	JUPITER	MARS
MERCURY	NEPTUNE	PLUTO
SATURN	URANUS	VENUS

EARTH VI — S4

Our planet, Earth, is part of the universe. Why is it hard for us to think of Earth as just one of many planets spinning in space?

EARTH

JUPITER VI — S5

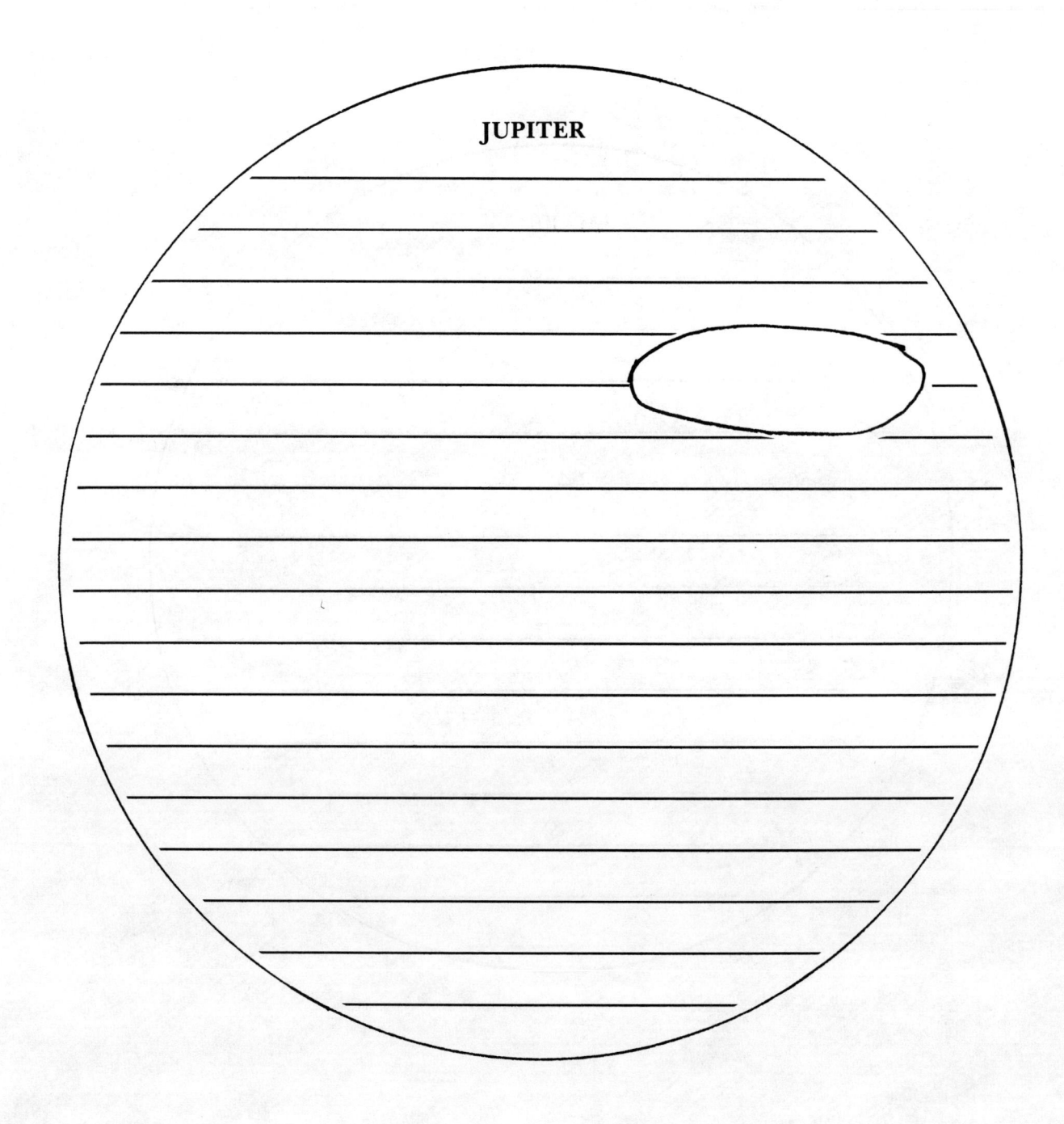

JUPITER

Who is Jupiter named after? How has Jupiter's big red spot been useful to astronomers?

MARS

VI — S6

MARS

_____
_____
_____
_____
_____
_____
_____
_____
_____
_____
_____
_____
_____
_____

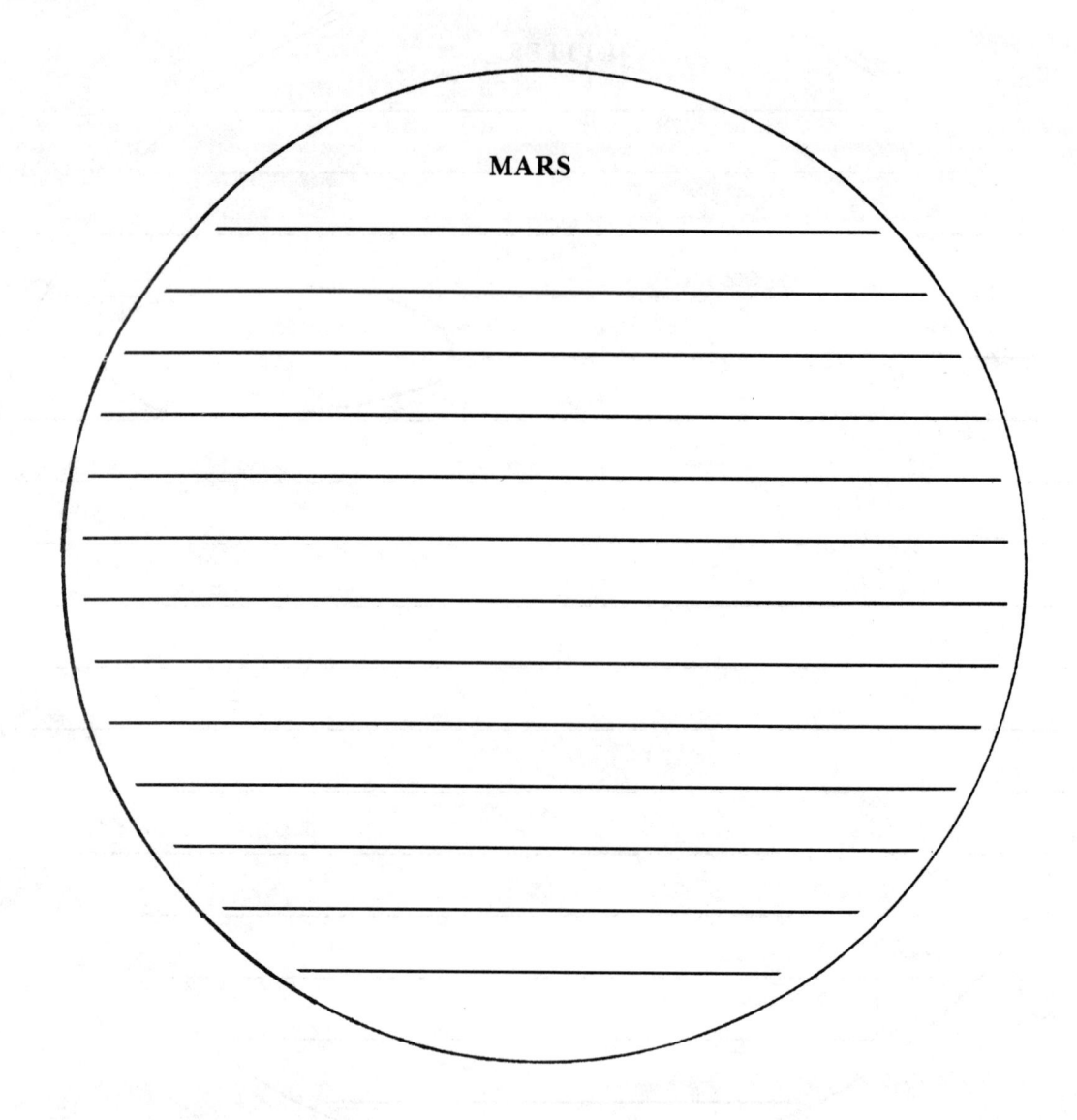

Who is Mars named after? What is Mars' nickname? Why do scientists think Mars has seasons?

MERCURY

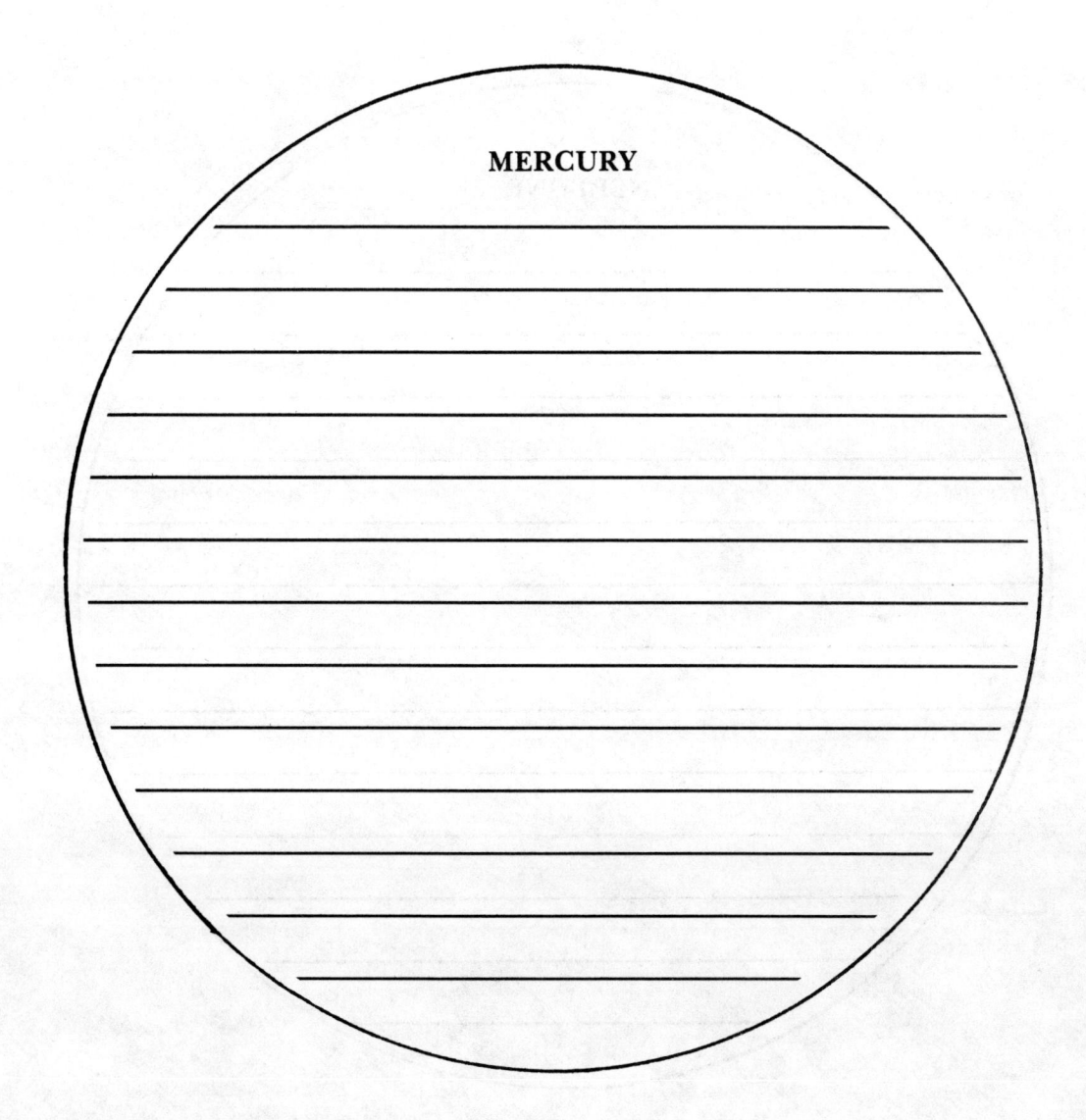

MERCURY

Who is Mercury named after? Mercury is the hottest planet *and* the coldest planet. It is always in darkness *and* always in sunshine. How? Why?

NEPTUNE VI — S8

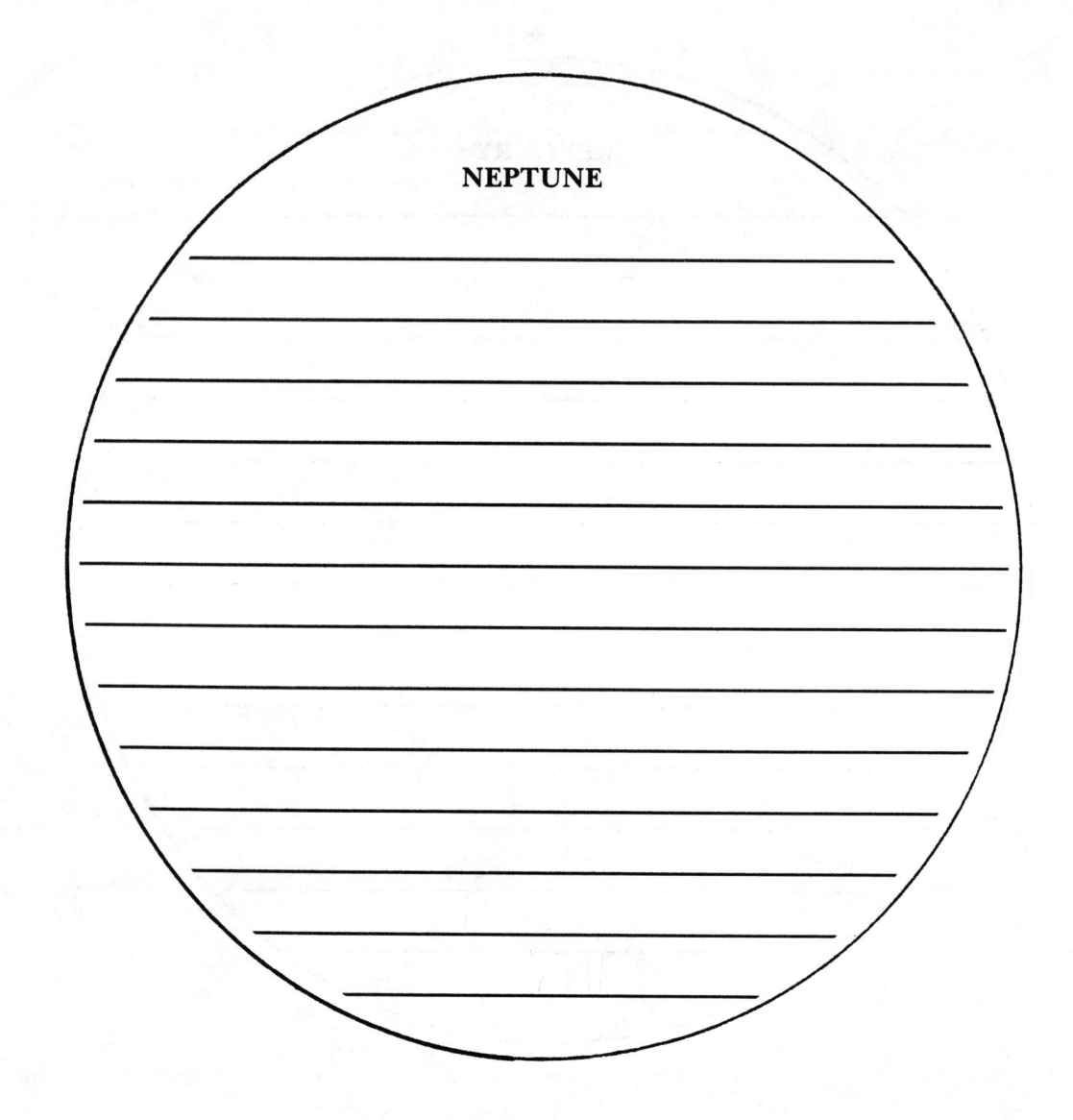

NEPTUNE

Who is Neptune named after? Neptune is one of two "green giants." Which is the other?

PLUTO VI — S9

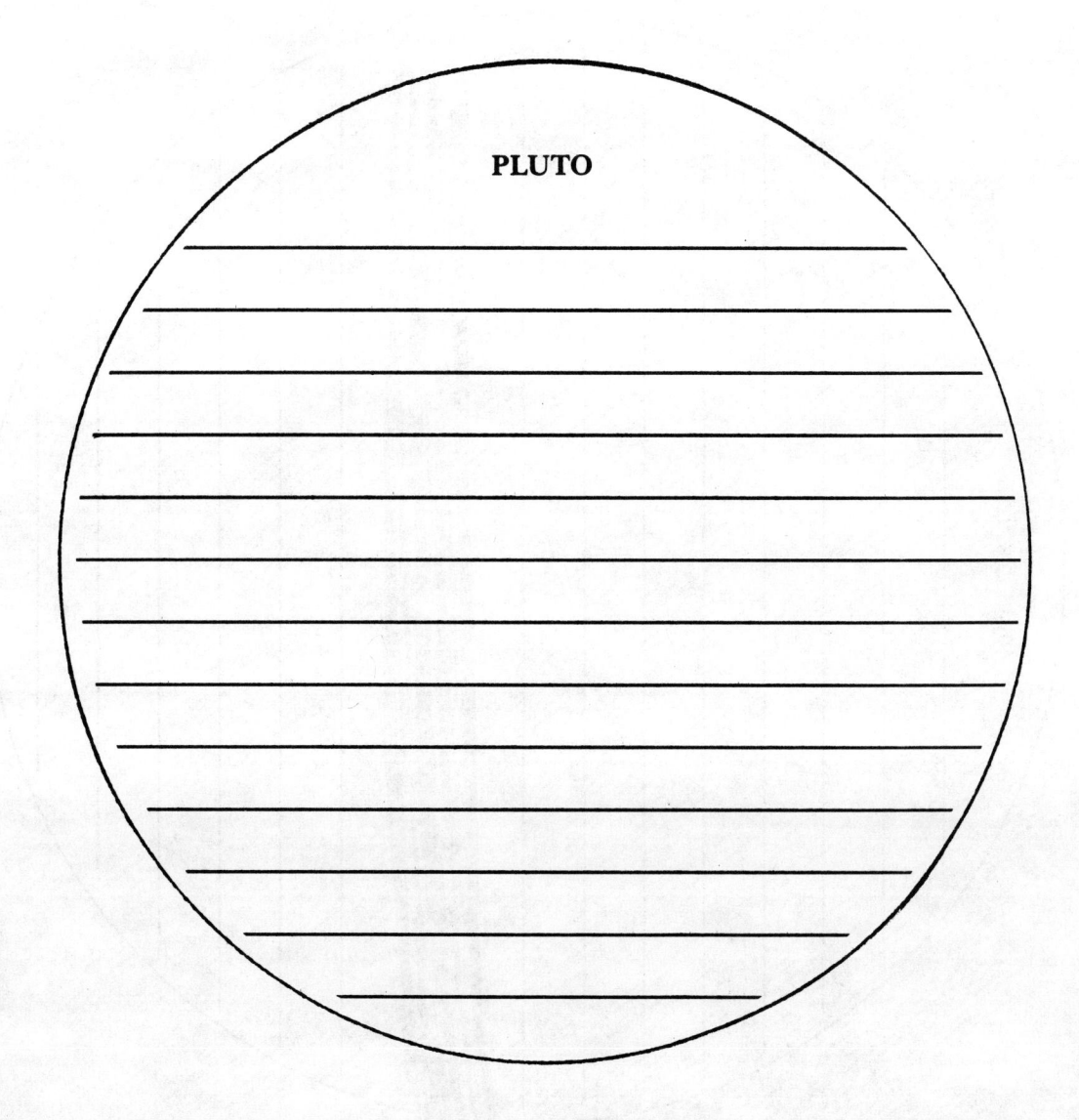

PLUTO
_____
_____
_____
_____
_____
_____
_____
_____
_____
_____
_____
_____

Who is Pluto named after? Why does this seem to suit the planet Pluto?

SATURN VI — S10

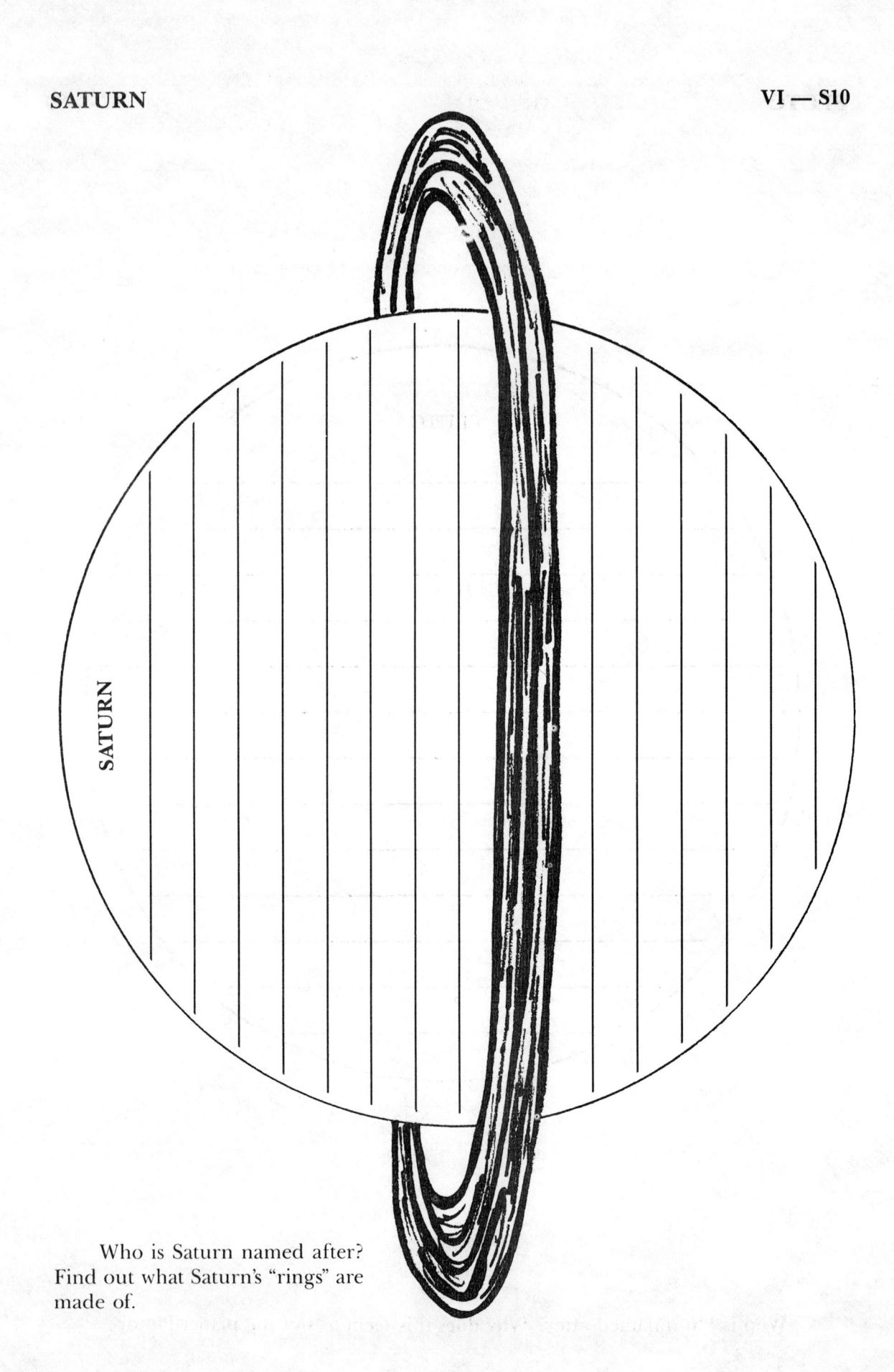

SATURN

Who is Saturn named after?
Find out what Saturn's "rings" are made of.

URANUS

URANUS

_____

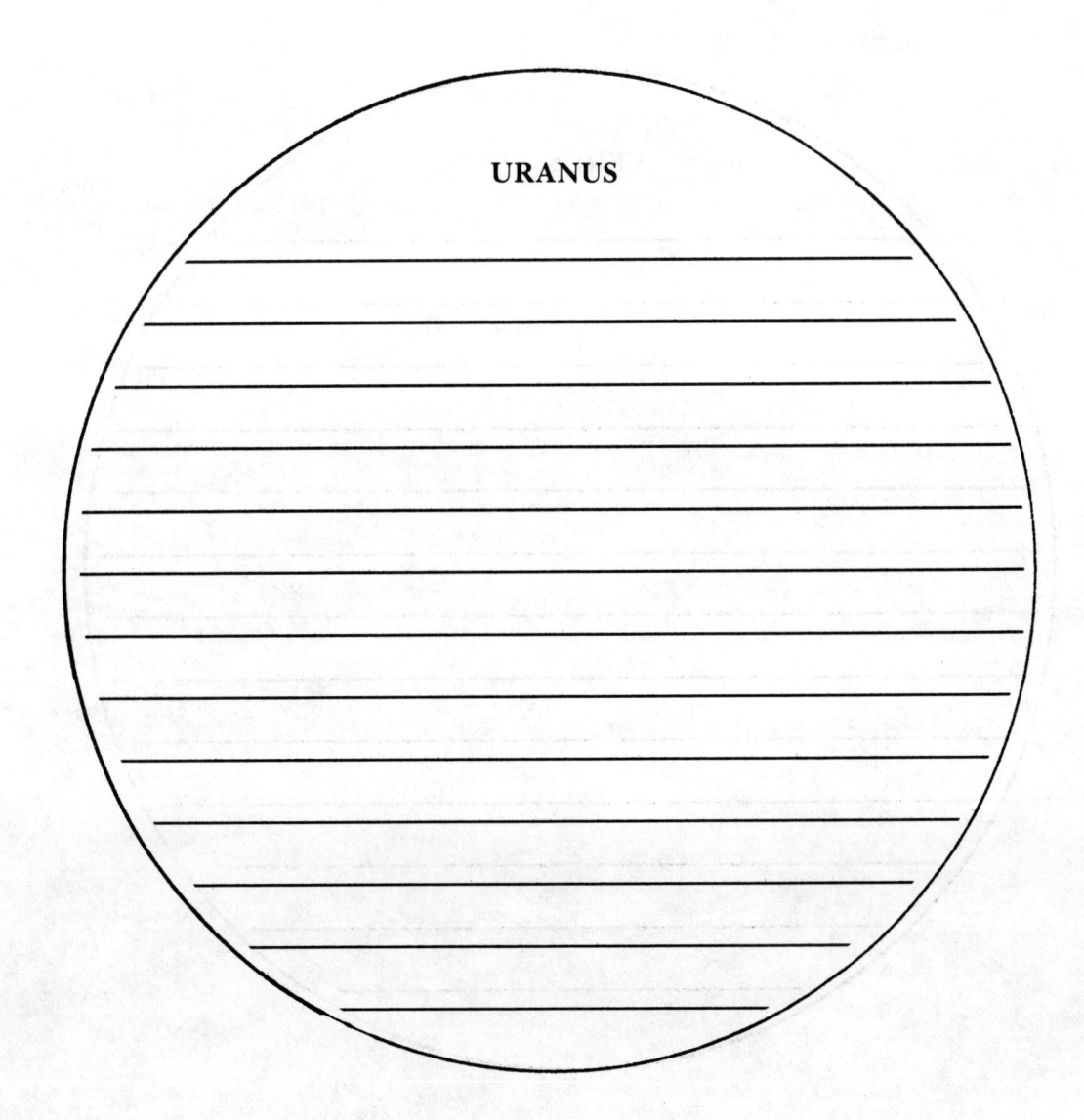

Who is Uranus named after? Uranus is the planet's third name. What are the other two and why were they changed?

VENUS VI — S12

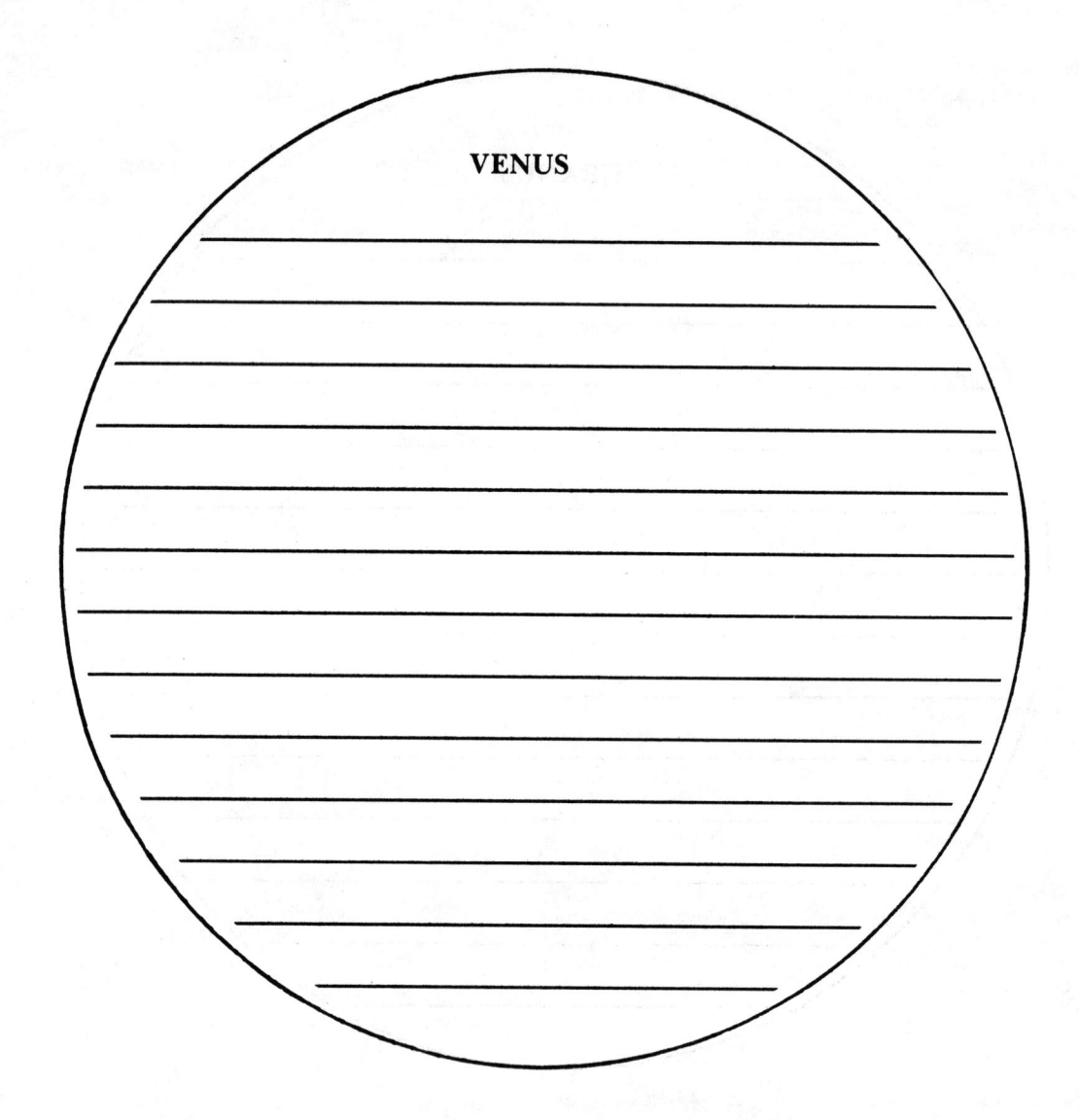

VENUS

Who is Venus named after? Why has the surface of Venus been so difficult to study?

SUPER EFFORT

VI — S13

1. Imagine you are from another planet. What would you think if you landed on Earth? What would you like to learn about? What things would disappoint you?

2. Which planets (besides Earth) do you think could support life? What would humans have to build or supply so that we could live there?

3. If you were to spend one year alone in a manned space station, what would you take with you for entertainment?

4. Make a hanging model of our solar system. Do the best you can regarding sizes and distances.

5. Use papier-mâché to make a three-dimensional chart about asteroids, meteors, or one particular planet.

6. Why is our sun such an important part of our solar system? Read about this and report to your classmates. Models and charts could be used to help you explain.

7. Our solar system is part of a GALAXY. What is a galaxy? What is ours called?

8. Make a mini-dictionary defining these terms: nebula, planet, asteroid, meteor, meteorite, comet, orbit, satellite. Add at least 10 more words of your choice.

VI — T

STAR TRACK

© 1983 by The Center for Applied Research in Education, Inc.

STAR TRACK   VI — T1

1. Check the sources you could use for this topic, such as books, encyclopedias, filmstrips, and pictures. Choose at least *four* sources and list them on Bibliography page VI — T2.

2. Study your project pages. Read and collect your information. Write the facts in NOTE FORM on outline chart VI — T3.

3. When all your information has been gathered, rewrite the facts on the papers provided. This time use proper SENTENCES. Proofread for spelling or grammar errors. Use markers, crayons, or colored pencils to outline, to color, or to do your own illustrations.

4. Cut out your outlines and glue them on construction paper. Make your star study unit in a booklet, a mobile, a chart, OR use your own idea.

5. See your teacher about making a SUPER EFFORT.

6. Present your work to the class as your teacher suggests.

7. APPROXIMATE TIME TO COMPLETE PROJECT: 6 — 8 hours.

BIBLIOGRAPHY

STAR TRACK

VI — T3

Name _____

Date _____

WHAT IS A STAR?

(Study page VI — T4 to find out the information you need.)

CONSTELLATIONS	OUR SUN — A STAR!

POLARIS — THE NORTH STAR	UNUSUAL STARS
	(Black holes, red giants, white dwarves, quasars, pulsars . . .)

WHAT IS A STAR? VI — T4

WHAT IS A STAR?

A star is _____

Stars seem to twinkle because _____

Stars give off _____ and _____

Some stars seem brighter than others because _____

The nearest star to us is _____

and the farthest one we know of is _____

In color, stars can be _____

Stars are different temperatures, too. For example, ___
_____
_____
_____
_____

On this paper tell what the stars are made of, why they seem to move, and how far away they are.

CONSTELLATIONS VI — T5

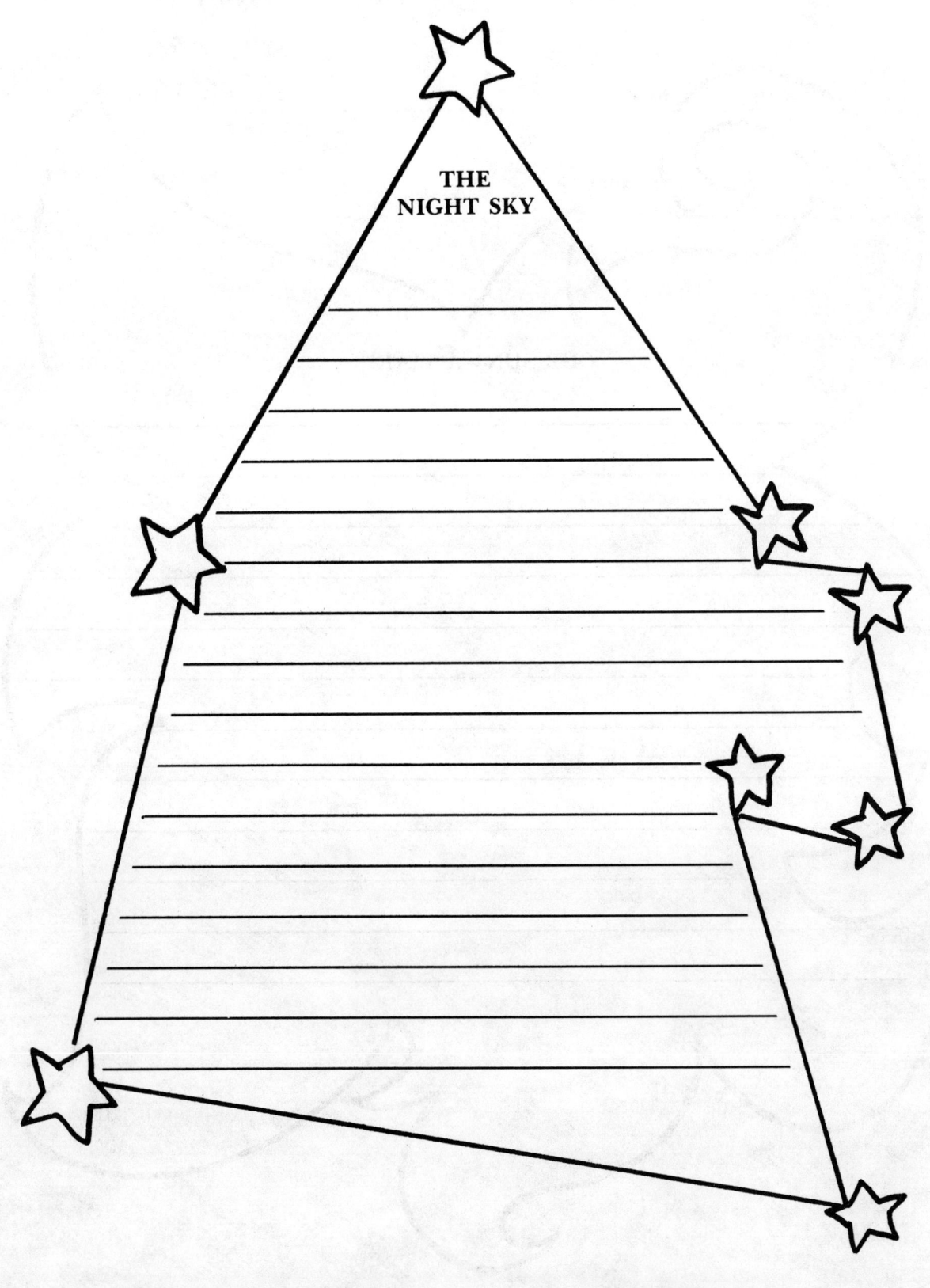

THE NIGHT SKY

Tell what constellations are and how they came to be named. On the back of this picture, draw and label some constellations.

OUR SUN—A STAR!

VI — T6

OUR SUN—A STAR!

_____
_____
_____
_____
_____
_____
_____
_____
_____
_____
_____

On this page write all the facts you have learned about *our* sun.

POLARIS—THE NORTH STAR   VI — T7

POLARIS—THE NORTH STAR

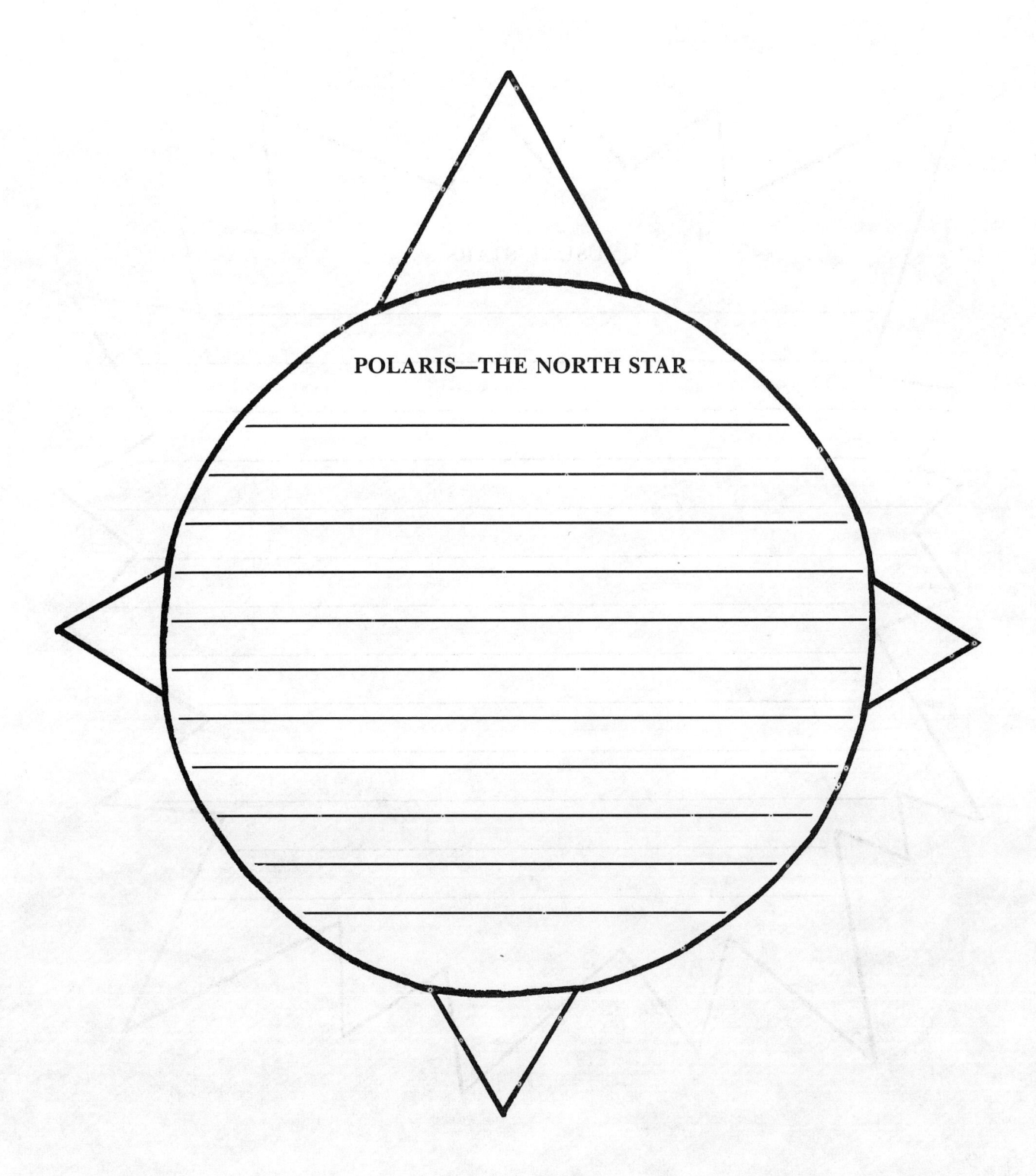

How long has Polaris been important to mankind? Why is Polaris still important now in the days of space travel?

UNUSUAL STARS

UNUSUAL STARS

Find out about one or more of the unusual stars. What makes them different? What causes them? (red giants, white dwarves, quasars, pulsars, etc.)

SUPER EFFORT

1. Read about PHOTOSYNTHESIS. Write a report on your findings to give to your classmates.

2. Some early peoples worshipped the sun. Read about one or more of these peoples and report on your findings.

3. What is an ECLIPSE? Prepare a chart that uses pictures and explanations to illustrate an eclipse.

4. Some people believe SUN SPOTS affect many things on Earth. Read about this and discuss your findings with your teacher.

5. Make a model (hanging or standing) that shows the Earth, the moon, and the sun in space.

6. What causes a rainbow? Do you think there is really a pot of gold at the end? Do you think wishing on rainbows really works? Explain your answers.

7. Write a descriptive paragraph that tells what the sun's surface would look like *if* you could see it from one mile away.

8. If you read the newspaper headline, OUR SUN IS DYING, what would you do?

VI — W

WEATHER

WEATHER   VI — W1

1. Check the sources you could use for this topic, such as books, encyclopedias, filmstrips, and pictures. Choose at least four sources and list them on Bibliography page VI — W2.

2. Study your project pages. Read and collect the information you need. Write the information in NOTE FORM on outline charts VI — W3 and VI — W4.

3. When you have gathered all your facts, rewrite your information on the outline pages. Use proper SENTENCES. Check for spelling or grammar errors. Use markers, crayons, or colored pencils to outline or color the pictures.

4. Cut out the outlines and glue them on construction paper. Make your weather unit into a booklet, a mobile, a chart, OR use your own idea.

5. See your teacher about making a SUPER EFFORT.

6. Present your work to the class as your teacher suggests.

7. APPROXIMATE TIME TO COMPLETE PROJECT: 8 — 10 hours.

BIBLIOGRAPHY VI — W2

BIBLIOGRAPHY

WEATHER

VI — W3

Name _____

Date _____

WHAT IS CONDENSATION?	WHAT IS EVAPORATION?

CAUSES OF:

WIND	RAIN	SNOW	FOG

CLOUDS AND THE WEATHER THEY BRING

CUMULUS	CIRRUS	STRATUS	NIMBUS

WEATHER

VI — W4

Name _____

Date _____

WHAT IS THUNDER?	WHAT IS LIGHTNING?

HURRICANES AND TORNADOES

HURRICANES	TORNADOES

OTHER INTERESTING FACTS

CONDENSATION AND EVAPORATION

VI — W5

WHAT IS CONDENSATION?

_____
_____
_____
_____

WHAT IS EVAPORATION?

_____
_____
_____
_____
_____
_____

CAUSES OF WIND, RAIN, SNOW, FOG

WHAT CAUSES

Wind? _____

Rain? _____

Snow? _____

Fog? _____

CLOUDS VI — W7

Cumulus Clouds: _____
_____
_____
_____
_____

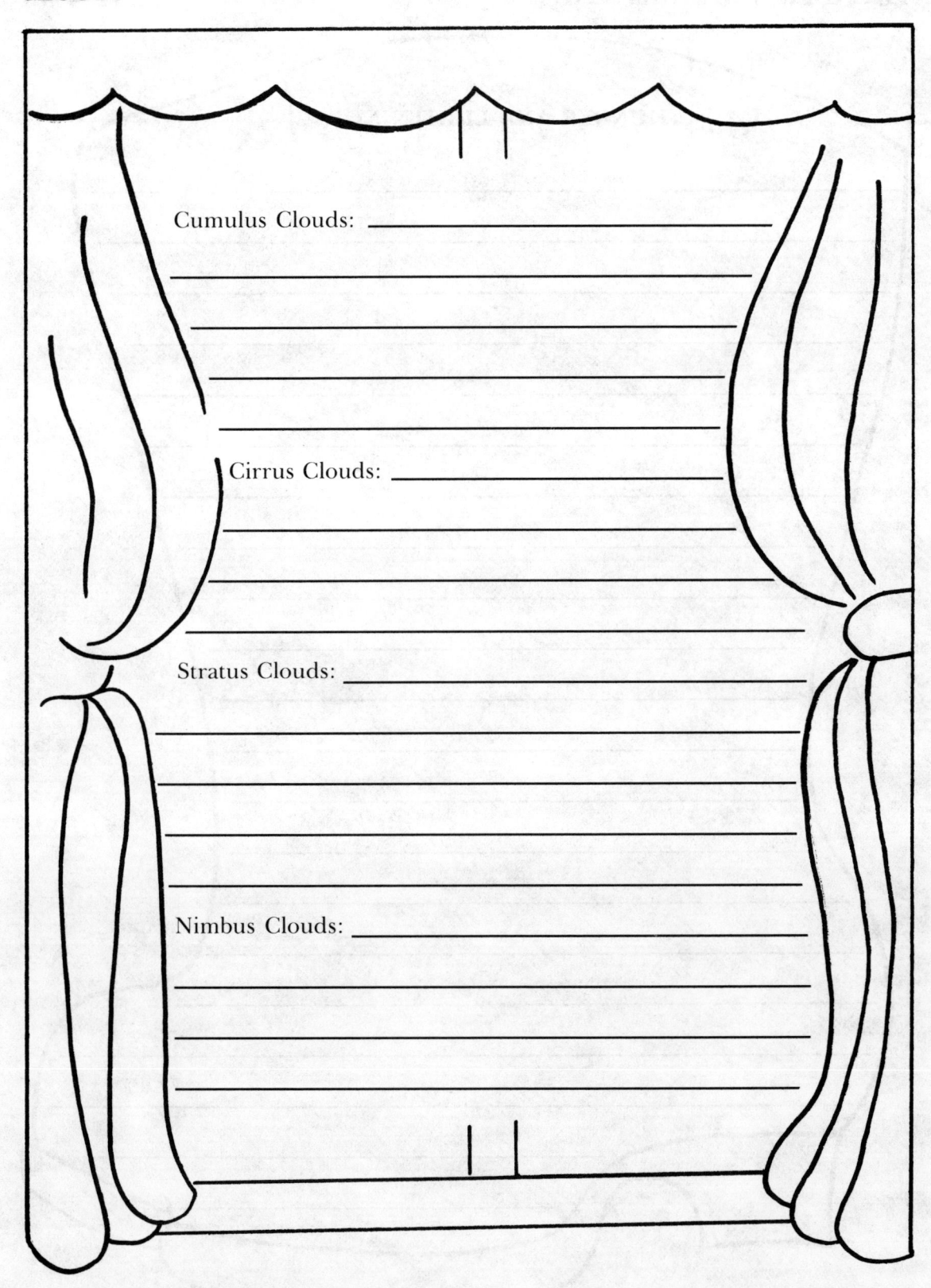

Cirrus Clouds: _____
_____
_____
_____
_____

Stratus Clouds: _____
_____
_____
_____
_____
_____

Nimbus Clouds: _____
_____
_____
_____
_____
_____

Describe each cloud and the weather it brings. On the back of this picture, draw an illustration of each.

CLOUDS VI — W7

THUNDER AND LIGHTNING VI — W8

THUNDER AND LIGHTNING

On this page talk about the causes of thunder and lightning.

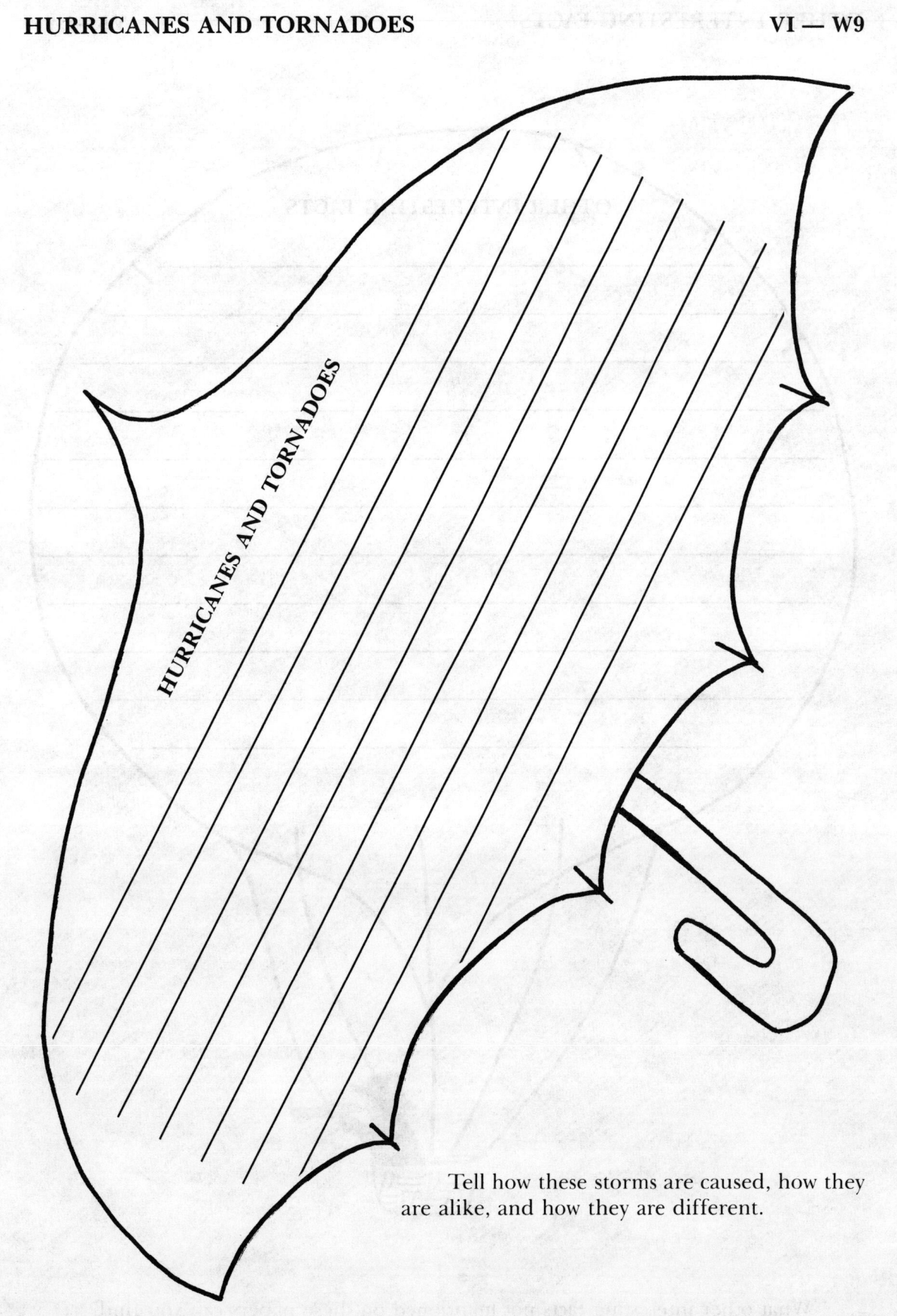

HURRICANES AND TORNADOES

VI — W9

HURRICANES AND TORNADOES

Tell how these storms are caused, how they are alike, and how they are different.

OTHER INTERESTING FACTS　　　　　　　　　　　　　　　　VI — W10

OTHER INTERESTING FACTS

_____
_____
_____
_____
_____
_____
_____
_____
_____
_____

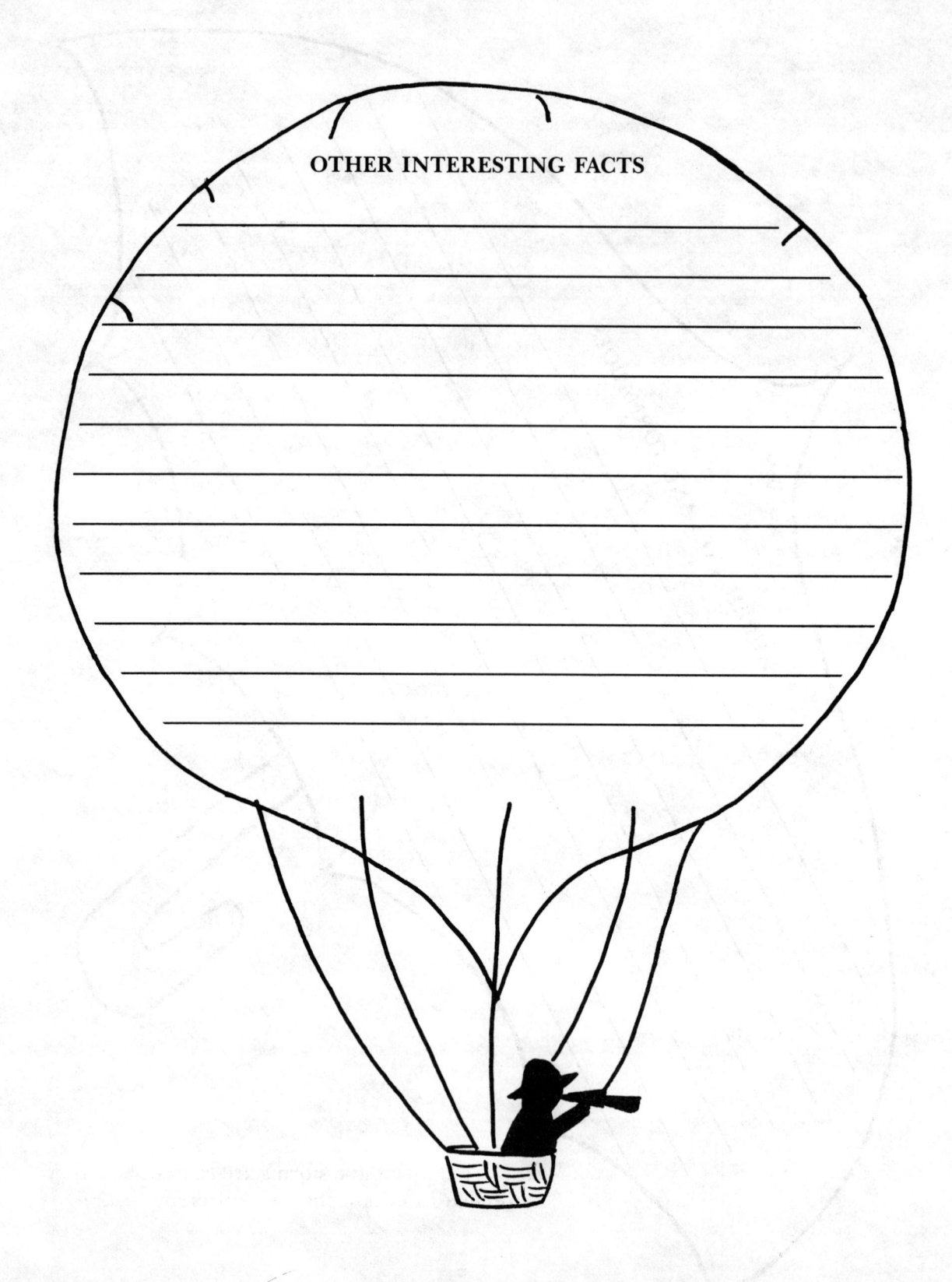

What other interesting facts not mentioned on these papers can you find?

SUPER EFFORT

1. What is a rainbow? Read about rainbows and what causes them. Is there such a thing as a "moonbow"?

2. Weather can affect people's lives in many ways. Write a story that tells how weather has affected *your* life.

3. Look at weather reports in a newspaper. Write some imaginary reports for special days, for example: the school picnic, closing the school, buying a rubber raft, or waxing your toboggan.

4. If you controlled the weather, what changes would you make?

5. Weather forecasters use many sources and instruments to forecast the weather. Read about them and describe one or two. You could make a chart to help you.

6. Floods, droughts, tornadoes, and hurricanes have affected people for many years. Read to learn about some of the more severe weather results and report on them (for example, the Dust Bowl).